BODY OF FAITH

By

LUIS ALFARO

Dramatic Publishing
Woodstock, Illinois • England • Australia • New Zealand

*** NOTICE ***

IMPORTANT BILLING AND CREDIT REQUIREMENTS

All producers of the Play *must* give credit to the Author of the Play in all programs distributed in connection with performances of the Play and in all instances in which the title of the play appears for purposes of advertising, publicizing or otherwise exploiting the Play and/or a production. The name of the Author *must* also appear on a separate line, on which no other name appears, immediately following the title, and *must* appear in size of type not less than fifty percent (50%) the size of the title type. Biographical information on the Author, if included in the playbook, may be used in all programs. *In all programs this notice must appear:*

BODY OF FAITH was first presented by Cornerstone Theater Company and the L.A. Gay & Lesbian Center (who first commissioned the playwright), at their Renberg Theater, Hollywood, Calif., February 20 - March 22, 2003. The production was directed by Christopher Liam Moore and included the following:

THE COMPANY

Abdulla Almuntheri
Donna Cassyd
Pierre L. Chambers
Nyra Constant
Peter Howard
Ebonie Hubbard
Audrey E. Lockwood
Michael R. Mallory
Ruben Marquez
Alejandra (Alex) Navarro

Stephanie Sarah
Debra Pasquerette
Ilya Pearlman
Adina Porter
Bennett Schneider
Loraine Sheilds
Leslie Sloan
Peter James Smith
George Weiss Vando

PRODUCTION STAFF AND CREW

Nathan Birnbaum . . . . Songs
Paula Donnelly . . . . Management
Daniel Foster . . . . Images
Rachel Hauck . . . . Set
Lynn Jeffries . . . . Costumes/Puppets
Younwha Kong . . . . Lights
Geoff Korf . . . . Lights
Ken Roht . . . . Movement

ORDER OF PERFORMANCE

In the Beginning . . . . Ensemble

The Book - One [Story of Sam] . Donna, Michael, Abdulla,
Pierre, Nyra, Peter H, Alex, Ilya, Loraine, Leslie

I Am My Own God . . . . Ebonie

Broadway Babies . . . . Ruben, Peter S, Bennett, George

Hindu Chant . . . . Ensemble

Pole Dance . Audrey, Ruben, Adina, Pierre, Michael, Leslie

The Book - Two [Sam Gets Wiser] . . . Abdulla, Stephanie,
Pierre, Nyra, Peter H, Ruben, Alex, Ilya, Loraine, Leslie,
Michael

I Saw God . . . . Bennett

The Circle . . . . Peter S, Stephanie, Abdulla, Pierre, Adina,
Alex, Loraine, Ebonie, Ilya, Michael, Debra, Nyra,
Leslie, George

The Book - Three [Fundamentally Different] . . . . . George,
Leslie

Womyn Only . . . . Nyra, Donna

Me, Just Me . . . . Debra, Stephanie

Ambiguous Girl . . . . Stephanie, Debra, Peter S, Alex

Ch-Ch-Ch-Changes . . . . Peter S, Ilya

The Book - Four [Lessons From the Quran] . . . . . Ensemble

5

* * *

The juice is in what you don't know
In the mystery that draws you down deeper
Marilyn Sewell, *Resurrecting Grace*

Are ye listening to me?
We are, sir
And what's enough?
The gift of faith, sir
Good
Go home
Frank Mccourt, *Angela's Ashes*

BODY OF FAITH

A Play in One Act
For a flexible cast - as many as 19, as few as 8

<u>CHARACTERS</u>

AUDREY
BENNETT
DEBRA
STEPHANIE
PIERRE
RUBEN
ADINA
GEORGE
LORAINE
MICHAEL
ILYA
ALEX (ALEJANDRA)
EBONIE
PETER S.
NYRA
PETER H.
DONNA
ABDULLA
LESLIE

AUTHOR'S NOTES

A NEW BEGINNING

A white space.

In some ways this is a space for light to reflect, but also for images to be projected. A space that can be womb-like or to be shrouded in. It might even look like a canvas about to be filled. Empty, like an installation.

Hanging from the ceiling on long thin wires are simple colorful sleeveless dresses. Those early sixties/girl-group types that can easily be sewn from a *Simplicity* pattern. They float out there. They are in different colors with patterns. They hang like bodies in the space.

Upstage there is a row of chairs that the actors will sit in. The chairs are in a semi-circle and face the audience. The performers will act as a Greek chorus, of sorts. But maybe also witnesses to the testimony this evening. In front of the chairs is a strip of floor lights. This will give the performers a *Brechtian* glow. This (it's all assumption, folks) will also cast shadows of bodies against the walls.

The playing area is a simple deck that is maybe a foot tall. In front of the deck is another row of footlights. These will create the feeling that this is a vaudeville. No, not a vaudeville, a *neo-vaudeville*.

To each side of the stage there are interesting matching screens. Very crisp in their design. They will frame the actors in silhouette as they change costumes. It seems that the screens also present the possibility that the actor is always present. Even when she/he is just in shadow.

The body present in transformation. Do the bodies change shape and form? Do they change gender? Is there a sissy form? Is there a butch form? Do the bodies become puppets? Only the screens will tell...

CHARACTER NAMES:
Use the actual names of your actors, select new names for each, or use the names in the script (which are the names of the actors in the original production).

IN THE BEGINNING

(A score that becomes large and ambitious and almost orchestral. Maybe it's something like, well not like, ('cause we don't want it to sound at all like that) but energetically like—"Song for Shelter" from Fat Boy Slim's "Halfway Between the Gutter and the Stars." And it begins to build as the actors enter. Bodies without commentary. Wearing body stockings (or nude, if possible in your production). They stand facing the audience and they begin to look up one by one heavenward. In some sort of ecstasy, we think. As they do, and as the music builds, one by one, they reach out to the sky. Hands going up in space. The dresses begin to lower and they fit into each body. They all get a look, so to speak, or maybe a gender or personality.

The performance begins.

The actors sit on the chairs. There is a moment of acknowledgment and silence. Then the company, one by one, or in groups, begin to clap out with their palms, a rhythm. Something gypsy-like that could support a choral recitation. Perhaps manifesting in movement? A dance at the chairs while sitting? Bodies moving in space/through scrims? Who knows, I just write it.

And so it starts. A kind of tribal song/chant. And, so, this is one of the elements that will be present in the performance. A kind of song cycle that underscores or introduces monologues and scenes.

AUDREY
   In the beginning.

ENSEMBLE
   In the beginning…

BENNETT
   In the beginning.

ENSEMBLE
   In the beginning…

DEBRA
   In the beginning.

ENSEMBLE
   In the beginning…

DEBRA
   There was the spirit.

STEPHANIE
   And the spirit was good.

PIERRE
   Because the spirit,

RUBEN
was holy.

ADINA
And divine.

GEORGE
And meaningful.

LORAINE
And profound.

ENSEMBLE
profound...

MICHAEL
And it meant something.

ILYA
It meant something.

ALEX
To be in the spirit.

EBONIE
The spirit.

PETER S
The presence of.

NYRA
A spirit.

(Beat.)

ENSEMBLE
And then came,

PETER H
And then came,

DONNA
And then came,

ENSEMBLE
the flesh.

ABDULLA
And the flesh was also good.

LESLIE
Because it was pure.

AUDREY
And full.

BENNETT
And it breathed.

DEBRA
And it gave a power.

STEPHANIE
Muscle.

PIERRE
    Strength.

RUBEN
    Movement.

ADINA
    But it was also,

GEORGE *(moan)*

LORAINE
    and,

MICHAEL *(thrust)*

ILYA
    and,

ALEX *(orgasm)*

EBONIE
    and it felt,

PETER S
    really

NYRA
    really

PETER H
    really

DONNA
good…

ENSEMBLE
good…

ABDULLA
to be in the flesh.

LESLIE
No, the flesh,

AUDREY
was good.

ENSEMBLE
was good.

(Beat.)

BENNETT
But not everybody felt good about,

DEBRA *(moan)*

STEPHANIE *(thrust)*

PIERRE *(orgasm)*

RUBEN
And somebody,

ADINA
  I don't know who.

GEORGE
  I ain't saying.

LORAINE
  No, no, not me.

MICHAEL
  Separated the…

ILYA
  spirit and the…

ALEX
  flesh.

EBONIE
  And they haven't been seen,

PETER S
  together since.

ENSEMBLE
  Until now…

  (Beat.)

LORAINE
  And we just jumped,

DEBRA
    a few thousand years of history,

NYRA
    to tell you a story.

PIERRE
    A new story.

LESLIE
    About this idea,

AUDREY
    of connecting,

DONNA
    the spirit,

ENSEMBLE
    the spirit,

ADINA
    and the flesh.

ENSEMBLE
    The flesh.

ILYA
    Out of necessity.

EBONIE
    Out of survival.

LESLIE
    Out of ignorance.

LORAINE
    Or complete intellectual curiosity.

    (Beat.)

ENSEMBLE
    I have a story,

RUBEN
    about separations,

ALEX
    and connections,

ABDULLA
    and desires

STEPHANIE
    and commitments.

PETER H
    Of moments.

BENNETT
    Of having been,

MICHAEL
    down on my knees.

PETER S
> And not just to pray.

(Beat.)

GEORGE
> I am the spirit.

LORAINE
> I am the spirit.

DONNA
> I am the spirit.

DEBRA
> And I am the flesh.

EBONIE
> The flesh.

AUDREY
> The flesh.

ABDULLA
> Stories.

ALEX
> Sometimes separate.

PETER H
> But tonight combined.

STEPHANIE
This is a...

ENSEMBLE
story.

AUDREY / BENNETT / DEBRA
Stories about...

STEPHANIE / PIERRE / RUBEN / ADINA
how people...

GEORGE / LORAINE / MICHAEL / ILYA
get by,

ALEX / EBONIE / PETER S / NYRA
In the world.

PETER H / DONNA / ABDULLA / LESLIE
Inside.

AUDREY / BENNETT / DEBRA
Outside of it.

STEPHANIE / PIERRE / RUBEN / ADINA
In one another.

GEORGE / LORAINE / MICHAEL / ILYA
In silence.

ALEX / EBONIE / PETER S / NYRA
With each other.

PETER H / DONNA / ABDULLA / LESLIE
  In a group.

AUDREY / BENNETT / DEBRA
  With a partner.

STEPHANIE / PIERRE / RUBEN / ADINA
  With a lover.

GEORGE / LORAINE / MICHAEL / ILYA
  With a god.

ALEX / EBONIE / PETER S / NYRA
  With a faith.

PETER H / DONNA / ABDULLA / LESLIE
  With a spirit.

AUDREY / BENNETT / DEBRA
  With a woman.

STEPHANIE / PIERRE / RUBEN / ADINA
  With a man.

GEORGE / LORAINE / MICHAEL / ILYA
  With something more.

ALEX / EBONIE / PETER S / NYRA
  Than just a gender.

PETER H / DONNA / ABDULLA / LESLIE
  Just my sexuality.

AUDREY / BENNETT / DEBRA
    The force of my identity.

STEPHANIE / PIERRE / RUBEN / ADINA
    With the power of a body.

GEORGE / LORAINE / MICHAEL / ILYA
    With the shape of my arms.

ALEX / EBONIE / PETER S / NYRA
    The strength of my hips.

PETER H / DONNA / ABDULLA / LESLIE
    The curve of my spine.

AUDREY / BENNETT / DEBRA
    The sweetness of my ass.

STEPHANIE / PIERRE / RUBEN / ADINA
    All that.

GEORGE / LORAINE / MICHAEL / ILYA
    And more.

ALEX / EBONIE / PETER S / NYRA
    Something bigger…

PETER H / DONNA / ABDULLA / LESLIE
    than me.

STEPHANIE / PIERRE / RUBEN / ADINA
    Nothing changes…

GEORGE / LORAINE / MICHAEL / ILYA
but the names.

ALEX / EBONIE / PETER S / NYRA
Everything changes…

PETER H / DONNA / ABDULLA / LESLIE
but time.

ENSEMBLE
Crossing bodies…

ENSEMBLE
crossing sex…

ENSEMBLE
crossing spirit…

ENSEMBLE
crossing flesh…

ENSEMBLE
crossing history…

ENSEMBLE
crossing time…

ENSEMBLE
crossing violence…

ENSEMBLE
crossing eras…

ENSEMBLE
    crossing silence...

ENSEMBLE
    crossing death...

ENSEMBLE
    crossing faith...

ENSEMBLE
    crossing over.

GEORGE
    This is

LORAINE
    a story...

MICHAEL
    about desire.

ILYA
    A search...

ALEX
    for something...

EBONIE
    bigger than me.

PETER S
    Or me...

NYRA
  bigger than something.

PETER H
  Looking in the temple.

DONNA
  On the edge of a knife.

ABDULLA
  In the earth.

LESLIE
  On the flesh.

AUDREY
  Inside the heart.

BENNETT
  In a spirit.

DEBRA
  I am remembering a story I heard.

STEPHANIE
  a poem I lived.

PIERRE
  a cross I bore.

RUBEN
  a god I had.

ADINA
a joint I lit.

GEORGE
a time in my life.

LORAINE
a prayer I screamed.

MICHAEL
a lover I felt.

ILYA
Some good times.

ALEX
Also bad.

EBONIE
Searching.

PETER S
For a poem.

NYRA
In the form of a person.

PETER H
A story that...

DONNA
became someone.

ABDULLA
This is a story about

LESLIE
story.

AUDREY
About.

BENNETT
How people...

BENNETT
get by.

DEBRA
In the world.

STEPHANIE
Inside.

PIERRE
Outside of it.

(Palms stop briefly. Palms start again. Rhythm quicker maybe.)

AUDREY / BENNETT / DEBRA / STEPHANIE
First I was afraid.

PIERRE / RUBEN / ADINA / GEORGE / LORAINE
I was petrified.

MICHAEL / ILYA / ALEX / EBONIE / PETER S
Thinking how I'd ever...

NYRA / PETER H / DONNA / ABDULLA / LESLIE
Live without you...

AUDREY / BENNETT / DEBRA / STEPHANIE
By my side.

PIERRE / RUBEN / ADINA / GEORGE / LORAINE
Then I spent...

MICHAEL / ILYA / ALEX / EBONIE / PETER S
so many nights...

NYRA / PETER H / DONNA / ABDULLA / LESLIE
Thinking how...

AUDREY / BENNETT / DEBRA / STEPHANIE
You did me wrong...

(Sound washes over palms...)

WHOLE ENSEMBLE
this is a story...
that is twisting.
and turning.
and shifting.
and changing.
and shaping.
and becoming...

(Actors begin to twirl and twirl and twirl. This could be a whole show that twirls and transforms. Maybe it can look like a Trisha Brown performance. An entire company in layered clothing that can become man, woman, transgendered, etc. Maybe have the women in the cast only play men and the men only play women. Okay, we'll see.)

THE BOOK - ONE [STORY OF SAM]

(Coming down from the sky is the spectacular entrance of a beautiful, but very simple, book. Someone in the company picks it up. When they open it they are illuminated from inside the book.)

ILYA
It's not a Bible.

PETER H
No, that would be too obvious.

LESLIE
And I am too young.

NYRA
In some ways, it's better.

PIERRE
I am on a journey.

ALEX
In search of a connection.

LORAINE
Between my knowledge

ABDULLA
And my spirit

(Two actors playing the same character.)

DONNA / MICHAEL
    I was born in 1951.

DONNA
    I was very interested in the sciences.

MICHAEL
    Very.

DONNA
    Maybe too much.

MICHAEL
    But that was me.

DONNA
    I was a precocious child.

MICHAEL
    In the fifties, you have to remember, it was all about space and new frontiers.

DONNA
    And we believed that we were the greatest country on the planet.

MICHAEL

The U.S. started a program called The Westinghouse Project. I don't know if anyone remembers that. But they started testing young children to see if they were of

ALL

accelerated intelligence.

DONNA

And I was one of those children that was pulled into this program. Sent to a neighboring town in Indiana to study.

MICHAEL

From my little town in Indiana with thirty-nine houses in it.

DONNA

At an early age I discovered a love of reading and books.

MICHAEL

I was split in half.

DONNA

Split in half in this program.

MICHAEL

To this day, my faith has been a journey towards integrating these parts of myself that I separated in my youth.

DONNA

My love of reading and spirituality.

MICHAEL

I became absolutely devoted to the Bible and reading.

DONNA

I started kindergarten during the Equinox, which is strange, you know. But stranger still is that I knew that.

MICHAEL

I was precocious.

DONNA

At nine years old, the third grade, I started noticing differences about myself.

MICHAEL

Well, I started noticing that boys were more interesting for me than girls.

DONNA

For me, I was feeling okay about it.

I was hearing stuff in church but I never felt that it applied to me. Because I grasped early on that Jesus ran around with twelve guys.

MICHAEL

And I was running around with all these young boys, so, it must be okay...

DONNA

So, I was in this honors class. And one of the things that we did is that we had an extra spelling activity where we would look up these really big words.

MICHAEL

And each week, one person from the class got to go to the library and look in the big dictionary...

DONNA

the Webster's...

MICHAEL

in the library.

DONNA

And I got picked.

MICHAEL

I got picked.

DONNA

And the word on the reading list that week was *homogenized.*

MICHAEL

H-O-M-O-G-E-N-I-Z-E-D.

DONNA

To form by blending unlike elements.

MICHAEL
To emulsify.

DONNA
To make uniform…

MICHAEL
And I am looking for the word homogenized in the big dictionary…

DONNA
the Webster's…

MICHAEL
and I don't see it. But, I accidentally find the word…

DONNA
homosexual.

ALL
H-O-M-O-S-E-X-U-A-L

DONNA
Attracted sexually to a member of one's own sex.

MICHAEL
Of or pertaining to homosexuality.

DONNA
A homosexual person.

MICHAEL
And to this day I can remember how my body lit up.

DONNA
There's a word!

MICHAEL
There's a word!

DONNA
And I thought, *there's a word for me. There's a word for how I am feeling.*

MICHAEL
And I went straight to the librarian, Mrs. Brook, and I say to her,

DONNA
Mrs. Brook! Hurry, hurry! I am in the dictionary. There is a word for me in the dictionary.

MICHAEL
And I take her over and show her the dictionary. and I point to...

ALL
H-O-M-O-S-E-X-U-A-L

(Beat.)

MICHAEL
And she is very polite. very quiet. very pale.

DONNA
> And she says,

LESLIE
> *What were you looking for, Sam?*

MICHAEL
> Homogenized. But I found this word. I found "me" right near it instead. And if "homogenizing" was good for milk, "homosexual" must be good for me.

DONNA
> And she says,

PIERRE
> *Sam, let's go see Principal Shirley.*

DONNA
> She is carrying the dictionary, with her finger on the page where the word *homosexual* is.

MICHAEL
> And she says to the principal,

ABDULLA
> *Sam found a word...*

MICHAEL
> And she opens to where her finger is, and she runs it down right to my favorite word.

> *(Beat.)*

DONNA

And he is very quiet. And they look at each other for the longest time.

MICHAEL

And they send me to the nurse's office where they lay me down and put a cold compress on me.

DONNA

And I am wondering what is going on?

MICHAEL

And while I am waiting there, in what seems like forever, I hear my mother's voice.

DONNA

They called my mother and she drove the six miles to pick me up.

MICHAEL

And I hear a lot of whispering, and crying, and my mother comes in and says,

ALEX

Let's go, Sam.

MICHAEL

And she drives me home.

DONNA

The next day at school, everyone was very concerned for me,

MICHAEL
and treating me like I was ill.

DONNA
It took me three whole days to finally get back to the library.

MICHAEL
I snuck in during the recess on my own

DONNA
because I wanted my word.

MICHAEL
And I went straight to the dictionary to look for my word. And when I got to that page,

DONNA
It...

MICHAEL
It had been...

DONNA
it had been

ALL
blacked out.

(Beat.)

MICHAEL
They outlined it in black ink, which I noticed...

DONNA
seeped to the other side of the page,

MICHAEL
right next to *homeostasis*.

DONNA
And I didn't know what was going on, but I thought,

MICHAEL
Wow, someone doesn't want me to have this word.

DONNA
So, later, I went to my local library, and the librarian,

MICHAEL
Mabel,

DONNA
I was her favorite.

MICHAEL
She let me go into the adult section because I wanted to read about,

DONNA
Egyptian pharaohs and Nefertiti.

MICHAEL
  And I go to this bigger dictionary and look for my word.
  And there are two references;

DONNA
  Oscar Wilde and Sigmund Freud.

MICHAEL
  And this was the beginning of a journey.

DONNA
  And let me tell you, Oscar Wilde was a lot easier to understand.

  (Beat.)

MICHAEL
  When I got older, I became a teacher's assistant at my
  high school. I would go to all these sixth-grade classes
  in the school district.

DONNA
  I would display little biology experiments that I would
  make for the students.

MICHAEL
  And I went to every school in my district.

DONNA
  And I always made it a point to go to every library. And
  in every library in that school system the dictionary had
  my word...

MICHAEL
blacked out.

DONNA
Blacked out.

MICHAEL
Every dictionary.

DONNA
Blacked out.

(Whoever is holding the book, slams it shut.)

ILYA
It's not a Bible.

LESLIE
No, that would be too obvious.

ABDULLA
And I am too young.

NYRA
In some ways it's better.

(Beat.)

PIERRE
I am on a journey.

LORAINE
In search of a connection.

PETER H
Between my knowledge

ALEX
And my spirit.

(The book begins to float away.)

I AM MY OWN GOD

(The company is spinning, spinning, spinning. All of a sudden a big bold lesbian breaks through the crowd, as they freeze.)

EBONIE
I am a dyke.

Not a lesbian, but a dyke. I hate lesbians. If it was up to me I would sink the *Olivia Cruise*.

I don't know, I guess I just don't believe in groups.

The truth is, I'm better when I am alone. And the other truth is that lesbians don't like me.

That wasn't always the case. There used to be a time when lesbians liked looking like lesbians. Not like Cher. We used to love all kinds of bodies. And shapes. And opinions. And ways of living.

I'm one of those old-time Womyn's festival lesbians. You know what I'm talking about? Oh, I love the hair on my legs. I love flat shoes.

I love a donut with my coffee every morning. I love taking a bath when I need one. I even love flannel, so fuck off.

No, them lesbians don't like me, 'Cause I like the wrong things. I love to smoke my cigars. Oh, I love me a big bloody steak once a week.

I also don't love a god.

There you asked me, and I said it. I think religion is a prison. I am my own religion. I am my own god. Don't get all Jim Jonesy on me. It's just what I think.

My power. My power comes from my fist. The power inside my fist.

Used to be I used my fist for fighting. The boys of course. There was always some boy's ass to kick. Then later the girls. Oh, sometimes a girl needs her ass kicked too.

Oh shit, I have been kicked out of so many bars. But that was then. Now I use these fists for loving.

I am one big loving fisting machine. Sounds scary, huh? But it isn't. It is a part of your body that is invested with trust and passion and desire and feeling and warmth and pleasure and eroticism and orgasms and heart.

Yeah, that's my fist. My power.

When I go deep inside of someone. The trust. The depth. The inner truth. I am looking at my God. Maybe me. Maybe us. Maybe each other's God.

Mostly I am looking at my own version of god.

So, take your god and... All right, all right. I can be fair. I can be fair because I have a little bit of god inside of me.

(She holds up her fist.)

Right here.

BROADWAY BABIES

(Two men, MARK and MARCUS, stand facing the audience. They are holding hands. Sweetly, or scarily, depending on how you feel about it all, they are dressed almost alike. They look at each other, kiss, and look back at the audience. The two characters are played by four actors.)

PETER S
Well, I think that God is everywhere.

RUBEN
Yeah, me too.

PETER S
He is in...

RUBEN
Everything.

PETER S
And

RUBEN
A lot of other stuff as well.

PETER S
Right, a lot of other stuff...

And I believe that because, I never thought I would ever end up with someone like Marcus. I never thought to look for him. Marcus and God, I mean.

RUBEN
God and me.

PETER S
Right.
I mean, Marcus wasn't even my type. And he was kind of *mean* to me when I first met him.
I was doing a bunch of bad things.

RUBEN
Like coke.

PETER S
No…

RUBEN
Yeah.

BENNETT
Okay, yeah, but, honey, let me speak, okay?

GEORGE
So, you did coke. Just be honest. It's just coke.

BENNETT
Okay, I did coke. Whatever…

(He looks annoyed. He can't help it and it turns into a smile.)

And coming out here to L.A. was…

GEORGE
so hard.

BENNETT
Right. Honey, let me speak, okay?
And I just couldn't get a sense of what I wanted to do. I wasn't being myself. Like I was…

GEORGE
Ungrounded.

BENNETT
Right.

(Small beat.)

So, I was spending a lot of time in the valley at all these bars like *The Rawhide* and *The Apache* and…

RUBEN
Oil Can Harry's.

PETER S
Yeah. Hmm. Oh my God, that place.

RUBEN
Smells.

PETER S
Yeah. But it was fun.

RUBEN
If fun is getting drunk and going home with everybody.

PETER S
Uh, no.

RUBEN
Uh, yes.

PETER S
Honey, let me speak, okay?

(Breathes.)

RUBEN
Okay, but be honest.

BENNETT
Right, okay, I am being honest, but just let me speak, okay?

GEORGE
He gets all embarrassed about his past.

BENNETT
Okay, you need to stop...

(Pause. Awkward silence. They both look out at the audience. Each one right, of course.)

I thought this was supposed to be about God and faith and stuff. I don't understand why we are talking about this. It doesn't have to be about being *trashy*.

GEORGE
Okay. Sorry.

BENNETT
Forgiven.
I was working indentured-slave retail at the Beverly Center.

GEORGE
Tell them which store.

BENNETT
No, it doesn't matter.

(GEORGE mouths The Gap *in silence to the audience.)*

PETER S
I just wasn't having fun. And I should have been because all I did was fold, and stand at the door saying hi, and making sure nobody walked away with anything.

BENNETT
Anyway, one night I was out at the bars in the Valley again, and I thought to myself, *this is crazy. I am starting to know all of the people at all of these places. "Intimately." And I don't like it.* But I didn't know what to do about it.

BENNETT / PETER S
So, I went to West Hollywood.

GEORGE / RUBEN
And we hate West Hollywood.

PETER S
You hate West Hollywood. It's not that bad.

GEORGE
No, we hate it.

PETER S
Okay, we hate it. But honey, let me speak, okay?

BENNETT
And I walk into *Rage*.

RUBEN
Just the name of that place should give people a clue.

BENNETT
And there's Marcus standing up against the wall. And I
was *kinda* drunk.

RUBEN
Kinda?

BENNETT
And I asked him something.

RUBEN
If I wanted to dance.

BENNETT
Right. And he just *laughed* at me. Isn't that *mean?*

RUBEN
I did not.

PETER S
Yeah, you did.

GEORGE
Well, you were all drunk.

PETER S
And, sure enough, before the last bell could toll, he
came back to me.

BENNETT
Drunk and all.

RUBEN
I knew what I was doing.

PETER S
Right. And we danced how many dances?

GEORGE
Just one.

BENNETT
Right.

BENNETT / PETER S
Just one.

BENNETT
Just one dance and he grabbed me by my hand and led me out to his car.

PETER S
And I was like, *okay, whatever...*
and I moved in within a couple of days.

GEORGE
Into my *small* apartment...

PETER S
Right.
So, God is even at *Rage*.

GEORGE
Not at *Rage. Rage* is a godless place.

BENNETT
And it was just so...

RUBEN
Easy.

BENNETT
Right.

PETER S

And everything he says makes me laugh.

BENNETT

And we like the same things.

PETER S

And our goals are the same.

BENNETT

And we don't argue, ever.

PETER S

And we just have a good time.

BENNETT

And just like that, I thought, *this is it.*

PETER S

We haven't been apart since that weekend.

BENNETT

Yeah, and this is how I know that God is everywhere.

PETER S

Because I just didn't think that something like this would ever happen to me.

GEORGE

Because you were drunk at *Rage.*

BENNETT
  Honey, let me speak, okay?

(Pause. He forgets what he is talking about.)

  Right...

PETER S
  Um...

BENNETT
  Okay...

PETER S
  Whatever...

HINDU CHANT

(BENNET begins a Hindu chant in praise of Shiva. Cast chants and dances onstage. They expand onto the Hanamichi and into the house aisles continuing to dance. Then, beginning on the farthest end of the Hanamichi, each actor begins to chant OM while striking a mudra [prayerful pose].)

ENSEMBLE
Idamava ēsivam (This, indeed is Shiva)
tvidameva sivam (Indeed, this too is Shiva)
tvidameva sivam (Indeed, this too is Shiva)
tvidameva sivam (Indeed, this too is Shiva)

OM.

[Pronounced: eeda may-va shee vum tweeda may-va shee vum tweeda may-va shee vum tweeda may-va shee vum]

POLE DANCE

(Five ensemble members stand on their chairs one by one. As they do they shed a piece of clothing. Maybe something not so obvious. A kind of spiritual stripping, of sorts. A sleeve, a pant's leg, a panel of a shirt. They each go to five different areas of the stage and perform their spiritual lap dances.)

MICHAEL

When I first realized that I was gay, I went to the priest, because I thought it was a sin. But my priest said, *God created all kinds of people all kinds of ways. It's the other things you should worry about. The other sins. Go on with your life.* I guess I was a minority in going to the Catholic church and coming out to my priest. The fact that I think he was gay too, probably made it easier on me...

PIERRE

I don't care about the dictionaries, *transcendence* is a physical word. When it happens to me, I leave my body. It's only bad when I am driving and have to find my way home.

AUDREY

The thing that happened with me was when I turned twenty-one, Kennedy was president. I was at a Catholic men's college run by the Jesuits. Even when I doubted that I was Catholic, I knew I was a Jesuit. They taught me *how* to think. Which is a very courageous thing to do, because they didn't tell me *what* to think. The most pain I have ever seen in the coming-out process is people who are raised in fundamentalist movements, because they are not taught *how* to think. They don't have the tools to deal with this personal crisis. This crisis of identity.

LESLIE

We risk our freedom by being authentic. Hiding who we are from the light is agreeing that who we are is evil. If we come out, we come out because we have to be authentic. And that authenticity will frighten any institution. Not just the church...

RUBEN

I made my peace with the Catholic church. I needed to go back. I missed it. I don't agree with the Vatican, but there are parts of the church that give me a comfort. So, I need to forgive what I can and accept that I am a Catholic.

ADINA

I think it is sex. And I think more than sex, it is bodies. That we are *incarnate*. Throughout history, faith has been an anti-physical thing. The spirit versus flesh. It's a whole dualistic way of looking at things. What we are doing is integrating sexuality and spirituality. Because we are defined by our sexuality, the only way we can be spiritual, is by integrating those things, and that scares people. Because they didn't know we could do that.

THE BOOK - TWO [SAM GETS WISER]

(Coming down from the sky is, once again, the spectacular entrance of a beautiful, but very simple, book. Someone in the company picks it up. When they open it they are illuminated from inside the book.)

ILYA
It's not a Bible.

PETER H
No, that would be too obvious.

LESLIE
And I am too young.

NYRA
In some ways, it's better.

PIERRE
I am on a journey.

LORAINE
In search of a connection.

ALEX
Between my knowledge

MICHAEL
And my spirit

61

(Two actors playing the same character.)

STEPHANIE / ABDULLA
In case you forgot…

STEPHANIE
I was born in 1951.

ABDULLA
But I am older now.

STEPHANIE
Yes, I am twelve.

ABDULLA
I am still a precocious child.

STEPHANIE
I became devoted to the Bible and reading.

ABDULLA
The summer after the sixth grade…

STEPHANIE
I went to my first Christian youth camp.

ABDULLA
And I won the Bible drill.

STEPHANIE
Of course.

ABDULLA
Of course.

STEPHANIE
And I won a little book…

ABDULLA
God's Word for the World.

STEPHANIE
And I thought,

ABDULLA
Oh wow, a book that God wrote.

STEPHANIE
And I opened it up…

ABDULLA
and it was *John 3:16* in a hundred languages.

STEPHANIE
No problem.

ABDULLA
I knew some of the languages.

STEPHANIE
Of course.

ABDULLA
I remember Greek…

STEPHANIE
from *Alphabets in the Encyclopedia.*

ABDULLA
And I knew some of the Spanish.

STEPHANIE
And I saw that it was also in Chinese.

ABDULLA
and I thought…

STEPHANIE
that can't be!

ABDULLA
There are no letters in Chinese.

STEPHANIE
The symbols stand for words.

ABDULLA
And I started to freak out.

STEPHANIE
And I thought…

ABDULLA
Oh my God…

STEPHANIE
we're not reading the word of God.

ABDULLA
We're not reading the word of God.

STEPHANIE
We are reading a translation.

ABDULLA
We are reading somebody else's version.

STEPHANIE
the King James Bible...

ABDULLA
Scofield Edition...

STEPHANIE
wasn't the way that Christ wrote it.

ABDULLA
Was not the real word of God.

STEPHANIE
I started to study languages.

ABDULLA
I collected alphabets.

STEPHANIE
I was reading...

ABDULLA
a passage celebrating faith, hope and love...

STEPHANIE
or charity,

ABDULLA
if you are reading the King James Edition.

STEPHANIE
I read this footnote in the Scofield Edition...

ABDULLA
that said that the word used is love...

STEPHANIE
but it has been decided to use *charity*...

ABDULLA
to avoid the libertine excesses of the early church...

STEPHANIE
Libertine?

ABDULLA
I'm gonna have to look that up.

STEPHANIE
In the Webster's.

I SAW GOD

(Ooh baby, something happens with the lights that puts us right back there at the disco of our youth. The smell of poppers in the air and some beat, straight out of Giorgio Moroder's head, and onto a New York club. Spinning into the scene is everyone's favorite club boy/disco bunny/hanging on for his eighties' life dancer.)

BENNETT
Sister, I saw God.

Oh yeah, baby, I saw God everywhere back then. Because that's the thing about the seventies and eighties, God was so present.

I saw him at *The Palladium*.
I saw him at *Lime Light*. (that's obvious)
I saw him at *Danceteria*.
I even saw him at *CBGB's*.
And you know how hard it is to see anyone there, especially God.

I didn't even have a job back then. Just this body and all of my love to give.

It was disco that made me so loving, bitch. And I am not afraid to say that. Yes, DISCO. Spell it: D-I-S-C-O.

A *Turn-the-Beat-Around* disco boy, was I.

I lived for the clubs back then.
And things happened so magically.
You could be sitting on some couch at Studio 54 and
say, *Oh, I wish I had me some speed*, and out of the
woodwork, there would be Bianca Jagger with a Gucci
purse filled with *pharmacy*, baby.

I was at *Studio 54* on the night of so many nights.
The night Liza fell on the dance floor.
The night Grace Jones gave me a bag of coke because
she got paranoid.
The night Baryshnikov showed up and Nureyev gave
him attitude.

Oh yes, I was there. There in my Sergio Valente jeans. I
saw it all.

It was surreal.

I don't know if it was the start or the fall of the Roman
Empire, but I lived it. I took in every moment like the
method actress that I am, and I saw it all.

And anyone that tells you it didn't happen, is lying,
baby.

Lying through their teeth.
Because this was the most amazing time.
A time of *freedom and fucking*.

This was a moment in history when you could really be you. And if you couldn't be you, a little something in your system helped you believe that you could.

Because the truth is, I *flew* on some of the best shit. And I did not pay for one penny of it.

When I was flying I felt closest to God. To being myself. And, baby, I went for a bunch of rides. I flew on everything.

And joy was the state you entered into on the dance floor. It was joy. The way that bodies move when they are released. Oh it is emancipation of the highest order. To see someone hustle or boogie their way out of conformity. And sometimes joy became ecstasy, and those nights you danced because to stop seemed like sacrilege.

Oh, and I had a fan. Yes, I was a mother-fucking fan dancer! You know me, don't act like you don't. You saw me out there on the floor. This big old thing that I waved around with my petiteness. People be stepping all over each other just to dance near me. The fan dancer gives off good energy. Oh yes, she does. I sure did.

I lived. I lived through the gay cancer, bitch. I lived through the OD's, and the poverty and the disillusionment. I lived through hungry nights where I would stand outside the velvet rope of a nightclub flirting the doorman to let me in AND give me some drink tickets.

Because, baby, back then I was young and beautiful and I got so close…

(Beat. The feeling. It surprises him. Catches him off guard.)

So close… to that thing. God. Immortality.

And it really changed me. Made me a nun. Gave me a perspective. And you can say all you want, but I will tell you that the coke helped, bitch.

And in the end, that is what that era was—good coke, one-night friends, good feelings, the beat, beat, beat, celebrities and their admirers, the smell of poppers, skin against skin, sweating through a soul-train lineup at midnight and sometimes giving it up at four a.m. in some apartment on the lower eastside just so that I could spend the night.

It was the adventure.
The time.
When I was young, and beautiful,
and flying.

I saw God.
And he looked good.

And I haven't seen him since…

THE CIRCLE

PETER S
I believe that faith is the ultimate promise.

STEPHANIE
I believe that faith is the portal into real liberation.

ABDULLA
I believe that faith without God is selfish.

PIERRE
I believe that faith is adherence to the teachings.

ADINA
I believe that faith is a country singer, right?

ALEX
I believe that faith is what causes world wars.

LORAINE
I believe that faith can't be summed up in one—

EBONIE
I believe that faith is a good Scrabble word.

ILYA
I believe that faith is what makes people nail themselves to boards.

MICHAEL

I believe that faith goes well with red wine.

DEBRA

I believe that faith is meaningless. I am so lost...

NYRA

I believe that faith makes me want to search for the answers.

LESLIE

I believe that faith will never accept me for who I am.

GEORGE

I believe that faith is the last old idea in a very modern world.

THE BOOK - THREE
[FUNDAMENTALLY DIFFERENT]

GEORGE

I was raised Christian Fundamentalist.
We didn't worship saints at all.
We didn't believe in the Virgin Mary.
What we had was our Bibles.

LESLIE

I was raised Pentecostal.
I was raised in Baptist School.
I was a member of the Bible quiz team.
I knew the Bible inside out.

GEORGE

We spoke in tongues.

LESLIE

We spoke in tongues.

GEORGE

Cool, you spoke in tongues?

LESLIE

Well...I totally faked it.

GEORGE

Yeah, me too.

LESLIE

They never knew.

GEORGE

They gave me an exorcism to get the demons of homosexuality out of me.

LESLIE

Really?

GEORGE

Yeah. I was twelve years old.

After Sunday service one weekend, we were watching
TV.

And Tom Brokaw came on the air and said that it was
official that there was a gay disease afflicting men by
the hundreds in New York and San Francisco.

And my family got on their feet and raised their hands
in the air and said, *praise the Lord, praise Jesus, thank
you God for showing the deviants the way.*

I remember standing up and clapping with them, because
that's all I knew.

But, I think they saw the deviant in me anyway.

LESLIE

I went back home to Illinois after fifteen years.

Before I went, I logged on to gay.com and I went into
the chat rooms for central Illinois, 'cause I'm like, okay,
*hi people in central Illinois, where are you and what do
you do.*

I started chatting in the rooms and telling people where I am and what I do.

And someone goes, *Gail is that you?*

And it turned out be the former captain of my Bible quiz team. And we just started chatting about growing up Pentecostal and everything that goes with it.

GEORGE

And now when I read this book,

LESLIE

I realize...

GEORGE

I speak in tongues.

LESLIE

I speak in tongues.

WOMYN ONLY

DONNA
I am sixty-two years old.

DONNA / NYRA
I am Lesbian.

NYRA
I am Jewish.
I am Feminist.
I am White.
And I am progressive.

Faith is not really in my vocabulary, not in a religious sense at least. But, I am a believer in womyn.
And, that is with a Y.

I was raised during World War II in a Yiddish speaking, Chasidic Jewish household in the Bronx.
I remember going to shul.
I was upstairs with the women, who were crying, while the men were downstairs dancing themselves joyfully into a mystical state.
When I was in elementary school, this girl said to me, *You're a Jew and I don't like Jews.*
Every morning my *zadde* wrapped *teffilim* and thanked God he wasn't a woman.

I started out in the Women's Liberation Front in 1969.
I saw a picture of a Vietnamese woman holding a rifle
and a baby, and the caption read, *Join the Woman's Liberation Front.*
So, I called and someone came and picked me up.

DONNA
They wanted to make sure I came.

NYRA
That's how they did it in those days.
We would graffiti the city.
I once spelled *sisterhood* wrong and boy did I get in
trouble.

I am sixty-two years old.

...And I am so full of life.

I thank womyn.
For making me believe.
Maybe that's faith.

ME, JUST ME

DEBRA

Ever since I was a little boy, I knew that I was meant to be a very nice girl, but I had no faith that I would find the body to fit me, and I was destroyed by it.
I remember driving.

STEPHANIE

Driving through my small town.

DEBRA

I had just had it. I couldn't deal with having to tell my family.

STEPHANIE

I was in my car.

DEBRA

And I knew where I was driving. I was heading to a bridge in the middle of town. And that drive seemed like ten seconds, but later I realized it was actually like ten minutes.

STEPHANIE

It turned into a meditation.

DEBRA

A moment with me and my faith. Me and all of my beliefs getting ready to drown in the river.

STEPHANIE

And right before I hit the bridge, I thought to myself,

DEBRA

You know what? You better really think about this. You know who you are and you have always known. The next step has always been yours to take.

STEPHANIE

And it was at that moment,

DEBRA

that I realized that faith had gotten me this far. Faith in finding a body that fit me. Let's face it, my family knew all along.

STEPHANIE

It was just me. It was me that was not investing in my own my faith.

DEBRA

Me.

AMBIGUOUS GIRL

STEPHANIE
>I am *Ambiguous Girl*. I have dated women. I have dated men.

DEBRA
>I don't define any of it.

STEPHANIE
>*Ambiguous Girl* went to school to become a Jew.
>
>And then *Ambiguous Girl* went *shul shopping*.
>And I met a lot of rabbi's because, hey, I am *Ambiguous Girl*.
>
>And I met one who really liked me because I studied a lot.
>And I said to him,

DEBRA
>*My family is gay.*

STEPHANIE
>And he looked at me.
>I said,

DEBRA

My chosen family is gay. And I want to make sure that
they are going to be able to be a part of me here at this
temple.

STEPHANIE

And he said,

PETER S

Oh, we have gay people at this temple.
We have three of them.

STEPHANIE

And I said, *How many people go to this temple?*
And he said,

ALEX

Twelve hundred.

STEPHANIE

So, *Ambiguous Girl* ended up at a different temple
where the majority of the population is gay and lesbian.
But I wasn't sure I wanted to go there because I don't
just identify that way.
I am *Ambiguous Girl*. The Bi Girl.

DEBRA

The one in between.

STEPHANIE

Sometimes my temple feels too gay.

I mean, is this a dating service or are we here to pray?
More than anything, though, I can say it feels like home.

DEBRA
A home for—
Ambiguous Girl.

STEPHANIE
I know what I am,

STEPHANIE / DEBRA
By knowing what I am not.

CH-CH-CH-CHANGES

ILYA

This is what I know.

PETER S

The *trans* in transgender is also the *trans* of translation is also the *trans* of transformation is also the *trans* of transcendence is also the *trans* of transgression is also the *trans* of transubstantiation...

I have become me...and you...and I.

ILYA

This is what I know.

PETER S

I wanted to be a performer since I was ten. But being in a female body that wasn't the right body, I never fit anything. I got good feedback at auditions, but almost never got cast. I got put in small roles where my strangeness wouldn't be an issue. Like the undertaker's daughter in *Oliver*. I was awkward and big, but I couldn't sell that either because I knew I wasn't female.

So, they would always say, *you need to lose ten or gain thirty.* Ingenue or character actress. It wouldn't have helped. I wanted to be Gene Kelly.

ILYA

This is what I know.

PETER S

I made myself believe that I was just not that good. So, I kept not finishing things, like my body. I was trying to figure out who I was.

I was comfortable with the gay guys and I was female then, so I came out as a lesbian. And my version was *butch dyke.*

ILYA

This is what I know.

PETER S

I don't care about people's genitals.

ILYA

This is what I know.

PETER S

Seven years ago I started hormones.

I knew a lot of people who were transitioning and I would think, *why can't they just be different kinds of women?* Now that has turned into, *we are different kinds of men.*

ILYA

This is what I know.

PETER S

I was living in Seattle. I would go to this coffee shop, but not very often. There was this cute dyke behind the counter. And I thought, *oh, she's a cute dyke.* A few months later I went back and saw someone else behind the counter. And I went, *oh there's a cute... I don't know what that is, but it's really cute.* And then some months later, I went in and went, *oh my God, that is a really hot guy.*

And then later I figured out that all three of those people were really one transitioning beauty. And I thought, *oh my God, that's all possible. That's what you can get.*

ILYA

This is what I know.

PETER S

I was *okay* with being a lesbian. I was interested in men but it was hard to do anything because men perceived me as very masculine, and being a female still, thought I was a lesbian and therefore, not interested in them. You still with me?

ILYA

This is what I know.

PETER S

Saying goodbye to the chest can be hard because it's so much part of this culture, the breasts. But it is the most freeing moment.

There was a moment after surgery, still under the effects of the anesthesia, and there was a huge bandage across my chest, and I thought, *what have I done? A piece of my body is gone.* But it didn't last. Ten minutes at the most.

ILYA

This is what I know.

PETER S

The restrooms are an issue. Men don't care what you do in the bathroom. Women are very aware of their space and very conscious of who comes in and out. Public libraries, which are afraid you will steal books, don't put doors on their stalls. Those restrooms are terrible.

ILYA

This is what I know.

PETER S

Guys like me who transition can almost always disappear. So, I feel like I have to tell you. I have to say it. So, that people won't forget us. A lot of people disappear once they get the bodies they were meant to have. But I don't want people to make assumptions about me. Because one thing we do in our culture is lie about our past. If we are going to talk about anything, I can't say, *when I was a little girl* or *when I was in the lesbian community.* I can never say so many things about my past if I want to be completely in the male world.

ILYA

This is what I know.

PETER S

The *trans* in transgender also the *trans* of translation is also the *trans* of transformation is also the *trans* of transcendence is also the *trans* of transgression is also the *trans* of transubstantiation...

ILYA

I have become me...and you...and I.

PETER S

This is what I know.

THE BOOK - FOUR
[LESSONS FROM THE QURAN]

(The book comes in.)

ABDULLA *(chant)*
Oh, human being, do you cry for what makes me cry.
Do you see what has happened in this confused world?

ALEX
Growing up, everything was by ALLAH, for ALLAH
and because ALLAH said so.

ILYA
I lived for ALLAH and would have willingly died for
ALLAH.
And the Quran was his infallible words.

I prayed five times a day,
on time,
everyday,
in congregation,
because Allah said so.

ALEX
I fasted the whole month of Ramadan,
every year since I was eleven…no food, no water,
because Allah said so.

ILYA
  I never talked to the girls.

  (He laughs.)

  I'm never getting married…
  And all the beautiful boys…

  (He sighs.)

  were nothing but a tormenting test…

  I was no pervert and I was not going to be thrown from
  the highest building.

ALEX
  I read the Quran every night before I went to bed.

ILYA / ALEX
  I lived this book.
  My book.
  I breathed it.

ALEX
  Then I came to… America (Amreeka).
  Land of the free and home of the brave…
  and for ALLAH I will be brave enough to face America
  (Amreeka)…

ILYA
  I did stay away from the girls,
  I told you I'm never getting married…

but the boys, *ya allah ya allah*...
I kissed a boy, and then another, and another...
and then came the wine
and there went my prayers
and somewhere I lost my book,
but I found me...
gay ol' me...

You see, I'm not inside the book.

ALEX
I'm not outside the book.

ILYA
I don't practice what I know.

ALEX
I don't forget what I don't want to know.

ILYA
I'm beyond the book.

One of my favorite verses in the Quran is...

ABDULLA *(chant)*
And those who do Jihad in us,

ALEX / ILYA
And those who do Jihad in us

ABDULLA *(chant)*
we will show them our ways.

ALEX / ILYA
we will show them our ways.

ABDULLA *(chant)*
God is with those that do good.

ALEX / ILYA
God is with those that do good.

(ABDULLA starts chanting in the background and the ensemble follows.)

ABDULLA
Allah-hu, Allah-hu, Allah-hu

ABDULLA & ENSEMBLE
The floods (of hope) are blocked by fear,
And everyone manipulates hope,

The floods (of hope) are blocked by fear,
And everyone manipulate hope

Oh, human being, do you cry for what makes me cry.
Do you see what has happened in this confused world?
Despair manipulates with hope.
And shakes all my being.

GRIEF

PETER H
I am not well.

LORAINE
Me too.

PETER H
I have been searching for my faith.

LORAINE
Same here.

PETER H
My faith has been leaving me slowly for the last few years.

LORAINE
Why is that?

PETER H
Well, the closer I get to God, the harder it is to see him.

LORAINE
Why do you say that?

PETER H

Well, I have the classic story. I grew up Baptist. In strict religion.

LORAINE

Me too.

PETER H

I think it was basically when my mother died.
I prayed so hard to God. I said, *anything but my mother.*
Take anything from my life, but not my mother.

LORAINE

I am so sorry.

PETER H

I don't want the sorry. I just want her back.

LORAINE

Yes, I know.

PETER H

I was with her in her last days. She suffered a tremendous amount, but I was there. I felt it too. Her pain was my pain. I felt her presence and her leaving so clearly. When she died. I lost...I lost something.

(Pause.)

LORAINE

Well, I have been taking care of someone very ill for a long time. And it has been a gift.

Strange to say that.

PETER H

No, I understand what you mean.

LORAINE

A journey towards my own humanity.

It is amazing what we are capable of carrying, isn't it?

PETER H

Yes.

LORAINE

I have had a communion or connection towards the dead for the last few years. It's hard to talk about it without sounding like you have gone bonkers, but it's true. I think we all have had, just by going through a huge epidemic, we have experienced a connection to the other side.

PETER H

It is a gift.

LORAINE

Well, coming to terms with grief. It's so hard. I couldn't see the lesson in all of this in that fog of sorrow.

I mean, we had a president in the eighties who sat there and did nothing about AIDS. While 50,000 people died!

He didn't even say the word for seven years. I had an unbelievable anger and desire for revenge.

I remember one day a guy came in to my office. A financial person who was making a presentation to our department. And my colleagues started talking about Ronald Reagan. And I was horrified to hear the worship of this man.

All of this history. All of my experiences with people who had been ill. It all came to bear on me in that moment. Where was faith? Where was my faith?

PETER H
I don't know.

LORAINE
And the guy who was coming in to do a presentation was in this conversation with all of these people in my office. I was listening to this and I thought I was losing my mind. I really was losing my mind. We all had our suits on. This was a corporate situation. And I don't know what got into me.

I don't know what happened, but I got up and I walked over to him. And I grabbed him like this, ripping his shirt, and I took him by his shirt all the way to the front door and I threw him out. And he landed on the floor. And my rage was huge.

And I said, *I DON'T WANT TO HEAR THIS EVER
AGAIN. GET OUT NOW! GET OUT. DON'T EVER
COME BACK HERE!*

(PETER doesn't say anything for a moment.)

PETER H
What happened to your colleagues?

LORAINE
Everybody really flipped out.
I screamed, *IF THEY COME IN, HAVE THEM DO THE
PRESENTATION.
DON'T HAVE THEM BRING UP THESE SUBJECTS!*

I was dying inside. I couldn't take it. And I couldn't forgive.

PETER H
I want to have more to my life...

LORAINE
I want to have more to my life than the gift of seeing the
other side.

PETER H
I want to be able to experience happiness again, in its
fullness.

LORAINE

And I want God to know that even though there might be a lesson here, I really don't want to fucking learn it at the moment.

PETER H

So much weight.

LORAINE

So much.

PETER H

When will my faith come back?

LORAINE

When?

PETER H

When will it be okay to stop feeling the loss of my mother.

LORAINE

When will I be in the light again? How much can we take.

PETER H

How much?

LORAINE

How much?

(They both sit weeping.)

THE BOOK - FIVE [BOOK OF LIES]

(The book is floating in space. ADINA snatches it from the sky.)

ADINA

Not my story.
Not my story.
Not my story.
Not my own.

Somebody tell me a story I ain't heard.
Somebody tell me a story that could be about me.

Here's a tale that I want told.
Woman wakes up one day, and looks at herself, and says, where is my story?
No, really, where is my fucking story?
And she says it in a way that isn't angry so much as world weary and somewhat defeated, but honestly asking, *where is my story?*

Where is the story about the place where I went inside of myself?
Where is the story about the time that I was dancing in the light?
Where is the story about the time that man took something from me?

Where is the story about the time when my mama slapped me?
Where is the story about the first time I had an orgasm?

Not my story.
Not my story.
Not my story.
Not my own.

(She starts to rip pages out of the Bible and toss them on stage.)

Where is the story where the woman looks like me?
Where the woman is dark and beautiful like the color of a contemplative night.
Where the woman smiles and her teeth are a million lights that usher out the sound of joy.
Where her ass, the repository of her eroticism, swings and sways with the sound of her internal music.
Where is the story where the woman looks like me?

Not my story.
Not my story.
Not my story.
Not my own.

So why don't we stop lying for a moment and look deeply into this book, and say that the god of this book, who wandered the desert for as long as he did, never looks like he should. 'Cause, let me tell you something, if he wandered the desert as much as he did, he would look an awful lot like me. Like me. Then this would be my book.

There ain't no story in here that says we existed to do good. To feel love. To want each other. To say a prayer. To be ourselves. To be authentic. And real. And be ourselves. This book doesn't say that.

Not my story.
Not my story.
Not my story.
Not my own.

So somebody. Anybody. Everybody. Get real about these damn books. They don't say anything that we don't already know about how they all feel about us. Stop lap-dogging your way into their book. I want a book that I don't have to translate.

I want a book that has me as the lead. That shows the small of a woman's back. That shows the gentle caress of two women loving each other. That stops pretending to be. That cares enough to say something. Somebody. Anybody. Everybody. Stop lying. And make these books real. Make them mean something.

Not my story.
Not my story.
Not my story.
Not my own.

THE BOOK - SIX [SO IT SAYS]

PETER H

If a man lies with a male as with a woman, both of them have committed an abomination; they shall be put to death; their blood is upon them.

LORAINE

A woman shall not wear a man's apparel, nor shall a man put on a woman's garment; for whoever does such things is abhorrent to the Lord your God.

ILYA

Consider the work of God; who can make straight what he has made crooked?

ALEX

I am black and beautiful, o daughters of Jerusalem, like the tents of Kedar, like the curtains of Solomon.

LESLIE

Do not judge, so that you may not be judged.

GEORGE

Jonathan made David swear again by his love for him; for he loved him as he loved his own life.

AUDREY

Owe no one anything, except to love one another; for the one who loves another has fulfilled the law.

DEBRA

There is no longer Jew or Greek, there is no longer slave or free, there is no longer male and female; for all of you are one.

ABDULLA

Which of us can say what the gods hold wicked?

BENNETT

I like your Christ, I do not like your Christians. Your Christian are so unlike your Christ.

MICHAEL

Faith is taking the first step even when you don't see the whole staircase.

PETER S

This is my simple religion. There is no need for temples; no need for complicated philosophy. Our own brain, our own heart is our temple; the philosophy is kindness.

DONNA

When I dare to be powerful, to use my strength in the service of my vision, then it becomes less and less important whether I am afraid.

PIERRE

Religion is for people who are afraid of going to hell;
spirituality is for people who have been there.

EBONIE

Nobody can give you freedom, nobody can give you
equality or justice—you must take it.

STEPHANIE

The only way that we are like straight people is sexually, we are most different in our spirituality.

NYRA

The altar, as in pre-history, is anywhere you kneel.

RUBEN

God didn't deliver me from sexuality, God delivered me
from guilt and shame—sexuality is the gift.

ILYA

It's not a Bible

PETER H

No, that would be too obvious.

LESLIE

And I am too young.

NYRA

In some ways it's better.

PIERRE
I am on a journey

LORAINE
In search of a connection

ABDULLA
Between my knowledge

ADINA
And my spirit.

BOOK OF LOVE [WHO WROTE THE...]

(The book dangles.)

LORAINE
Where is my book?

PETER S
Where is my story?

ALEX
Who is the character in my Bible?

BENNETT
I am...

EBONIE
Forty-five

DONNA
Twenty-six.

MICHAEL
Fifty.

PIERRE
Thirty-one.

AUDREY
Twenty-seven.

STEPHANIE
Thirty-eight.

GEORGE
Twenty-nine.

NYRA
Nineteen.

LESLIE
Sixty-two.

ADINA
Twenty-six.

ABDULLA
Forty-one.

ILYA
Twenty-seven.

DEBRA
Thirty-four.

RUBEN
Forty.

PETER H
Twenty-eight.

ILYA
I am...

ABDULLA
  I am...

NYRA
  I am a Gay Male Former Catholic Optimist.

DONNA
  I am a Lover of Women and a Believer in God.

STEPHANIE
  I am a Gay Lapsed Recovering Lost Exiled Catholic.

PIERRE
  I am a Bisexual Jewish Woman.

PETER H
  I am Female to Male Agnostic Deli-Jew with Buddhist
  Leanings.

LESLIE
  I am a Christian Gay Man with the Power to Create.

AUDREY
  I am a Yogi Hindu Drag Nun.

PETER S
  I am a Latina Catholic Dyke.

ADINA
  I am a Unitarian Universalist.

BENNETT
    I am a Queer Catholic and a Gay Agnostic.

ALEX
    I am a Black Man Gay Spirit Wish.

GEORGE
    I am a Jewish Lesbian.

EBONIE
    I am a Gay Spiritualist.

LORAINE
    I am a Beautiful Boy.

MICHAEL
    I am a Quiet Gay and Spiritually I Am Hopeful.

ILYA
    I am a believer in non-organized religion.

GEORGE
    I am Straight.

BENNETT
    I am an African-American Heterosexual Woman in Touch With Herself.

DONNA
    I am an artist.

DEBRA
I am worried about my future.

PETER H
I am very attached to my cat.

ALEX
I am going to network.

EBONIE
I am a dreamer.

PIERRE
I am still having a hard time.

LORAINE
I am bad hair.

RUBEN
I am not much style.

ILYA
I am putting myself out there.

STEPHANIE
I am going on nineteen years of marriage.

ABDULLA
I am having a hard time with relationships.

PETER S
I am too sarcastic.

ADINA
  I am always focusing on the negative.

ABDULLA
  I am disconnected from my body.

LORAINE
  I am coming into my own.

DEBRA
  I am a red diaper baby.

PIERRE
  I am in need of creative energy to breathe.

NYRA
  I am angry at traffic.

LESLIE
  I am searching for a partner with new definitions.

GEORGE
  I am sexual.

STEPHANIE
  I am outspoken.

NYRA
  I am not particularly spiritual.

PETER S
  I am allergic.

BENNETT
I am down casual.

RUBEN
I am petite.

ADINA
I am Connie's son.

MICHAEL
I am a person overcoming childhood.

AUDREY
I am sometimes afraid of myself.

EBONIE
I am more talented than I let myself believe.

DONNA
I am not very good at staying in touch with people.

ALEX
I am giving, caring, greedy and selfish.

ADINA
I am really bloody wonderful, no, really.

PETER H
I am my breath.

LORAINE
I am a total sensation of love.

ALL
I am a total sensation of love.

PIERRE
I am always questioning.

ILYA
I am the community that loves me.

MICHAEL
I am comfort of prayer.

ALEX
I am the strength of my will.

RUBEN
I am simply existing now.

LESLIE
I am an outsider in my family.

ABDULLA
I am a person who is transitory.

RUBEN
I am crying in my mother's dreams.

DONNA
I am a recovered drug addict.

DEBRA
I am a person living with HIV.

BENNETT
I am a former homeless person.

EBONIE
I am learning to claim my age.

NYRA
I am a student of many faiths.

AUDREY
I am a beautiful boy.

PETER S
I am honorable.

STEPHANIE
I am nature.

PIERRE
I am an act of God.

DEBRA
I am reluctantly ethnic.

ABDULLA
I am only potential.

EBONIE
I am strong willed.

AUDREY
I am a lover of leaving.

NYRA
I am a sugar eater.

LESLIE
I am a weed smoker.

DONNA
I am a loving, giving African man.

PIERRE
I am "on" a lot of the time.

DEBRA
I am a worshipper.

PETER H
I am guilty around sex.

STEPHANIE
I am someone who doesn't like to work at looking good.

ALEX
I am Taiwanese.

PETER H
I am my mother.

RUBEN
I am a New Englander.

ILYA
I am persnickety, sometimes a snob.

ADINA
I am a gay, and I mean *gay*, man.

GEORGE
I am a confused artist worried about money.

PETER S
I am searching for a really good lover.

LESLIE
I am a daughter, sister and wife.

NYRA
I am terrified about living life to the fullest.

AUDREY
I am without a hero.

BENNETT
I am a Jewish Puerto Rican from Taos no less.

STEPHANIE
I am overweight and out of shape.

MICHAEL
I am in a relationship for twenty-seven years.

PETER S
I am a lost Catholic.

ADINA
I am a recovering alcoholic.

RUBEN
I am the third of four sisters who I sometimes compete with.

GEORGE
I am a relentless thinker.

DEBRA
I am a devoted spouse.

EBONIE
I am a woman of the 21st century.

LESLIE
I am a speaker of many languages.

LORAINE
I am Haitian.

PIERRE
I am worried.

BENNETT
I am improving.

AUDREY
I am basically good.

DONNA
I am open to new explorations.

ADINA
I am in my body.

PETER H
I am dancing in the light.

(Something shifts. Real people say who they really are. Simple. Ritual.)

ABDULLA
I am Abdulla Almuntheri.

DONNA
I am Donna Cassyd.

PIERRE
I am Pierre L. Chambers.

NYRA
I am Nyra Constant.

PETER H
I am Peter Howard.

EBONIE
I am Ebonie Hubbard.

AUDREY
I am Audrey Lockwood.

MICHAEL
I am Michael R. Mallory.

RUBEN
I am Ruben Marquez.

ALEX
I am Navarro.

STEPHANIE
I am Stephanie Sarah.

DEBRA
I am Debra Pasquerette.

ILYA
I am Ilya Pearlman.

ADINA
I am Adina Porter.

BENNETT
I am Bennett Schneider.

LORAINE
I am Loraine Sheilds.

LESLIE
I am Leslie Sloan.

PETER S
I am Peter James Smith.

GEORGE
I am George Weiss Vando.

ENSEMBLE
I am...

END OF PLAY

DIRECTOR'S NOTES

DIRECTOR'S NOTES